PAWLEYS ISLAND

poems by

John Stupp

Finishing Line Press
Georgetown, Kentucky

PAWLEYS ISLAND

ACKNOWLEDGMENTS

The author wishes to acknowledge the following online and print publications in which
some of these poems or versions of these poems first appeared: *The Pittsburgh Poetry
Review* ("Inbound"); *By&By Poetry* ("If I Could Write"); *The New Guard* ("How Tuesday
Began"); *Uppagus* ("On Halloween Milt Plum Gave Out Autographed Pictures of Himself
Instead of Candy"); *The Timberline Review* ("The Night Gene Harris Tried to Kill Me");
Rising Phoenix Review ("Snakeskin"); *Slippery Elm Journal* ("Lunch Poem for Peter
Laughner"); *The Pittsburgh City Paper Chapter & Verse* ("I Shook Oscar Peterson's Hand in
Pittsburgh"); *Long Dumb Voices* ("Poem Beginning with a Line by d. a. levy"); *Houseguest*
("Wanted," "Another Poem About Fishing"); *The Mackinac* ("Frontier Days," "After a
Hurricane," "Pawleys Island"); *Wraparound South* ("Old Postcard on Ebay," "Floating");
Inklette ("Thank God Robert Was With Me"); *BoomerLitMag* ("Relaxing at Camarillo,"
"New Rhumba" and "West Village Afternoon January 1974"); *Third Street Writers* ("Not
a Very Good Poem'); *Birds We Piled Loosely* ("Springtime"); *The Pittsburgh Post-Gazette*
("Fortune Cookie"); *Vending Machine Press* ("Colorado" and "How They Brought the Good
News From Ambridge to Pittsburgh"); *Sediments Literary-Arts Journal* ("Passing Through
Weiser, Idaho"); *Fried Chicken and Coffee* ("Angels," "This Morning"); *4ink7* ("At Small's
Jazz Club"); *Sweet Tree Review* ("Tide Chart"); *Cactus Heart* ("A Trail in the Rockies");
Flytrap Uprising ("Drones and Chanters", "Crab Trap" and "Salt Life"); *Goliath* ("Cooler
Music," "Croaker Story"); *Drunk Monkeys* ("OK Corral"); *The White Whale Review* ("I Saw
a Flounder," "True Crime," "January," "Change of Possession" and "32 Degrees"); *On the
Veranda Literary Journal* ("Sunset"); *SHARKPACK Poetry Review* ("Goat Island" and "No
Luck"); *Shark Reef* ("Fishing"); A Fish Called Wanda ("Happiness"); The Strip ("Genesis")

The poem "Goat Island" was nominated for a Pushcart Prize in 2016.

Publisher: Leah Maines
Editor: Christen Kincaid
Cover Art: Bette Stupp
Author Photo: Bette Stupp
Cover Design: Elizabeth Maines McCleavy

Printed in the USA on acid-free paper.
Order online: www.finishinglinepress.com
also available on amazon.com

Author inquiries and mail orders:
Finishing Line Press
P. O. Box 1626
Georgetown, Kentucky 40324
U. S. A.

Table of Contents

To Bette, Robert and Kathleen

THANKS to the following poets for their unwavering encouragement and support: Michael Albright, Joan Bauer, Jan Beatty, Jennifer Jackson Berry, Charlie Brice, Brianne Griffith, Sara McNally, Deena November, Kayla Sargeson, Dan Shapiro, Michael Simms, Bob Walicki and Michael Wurster without whom this book would never have been written.

I

Poem Beginning with a Line by Wallace Stevens

Among twenty
snowy mountains—
the sky is falling
on Cleveland
on Edgewater Park
on the frozen lake
white as a monument
to winter's falsehood—
cooking the books
cold as the stone in Garfield's tomb
the twilight sun
the hardened chill
of Christmas
an icy bullet in the back
for your trouble
these are the wages
of fuck you
a simple marker—
the stillness
the empty ore boats
trolling to Canada
the birds complaining

On Halloween Milt Plum Gave Out Autographed Pictures of Himself Instead of Candy

An outrage—
on a night cold as the Arctic
he invited us in
hands trembling
as he dropped his image
in a paper bag
the 1959 Cleveland Browns uniform
lost in the fumbled dark
and no candy—
here you go
he said—
we mumbled thank you
and walked slowly off the porch
like plumed tin soldiers on
parade
trooping the colors
but nothing explained—
only the adult world
as always
inscrutable
unsung
a winter photograph
beneath leafless branches—
and snow starting to fall
like shrapnel
on the lake
on the city

How Tuesday Began

for MS

A marine sniper
young and tan
with his shirt off
tattoos and a short haircut
is back in the USA
and means business—
he is in the front seat
of a '71 Lincoln
pulled over on a tree lawn in Cleveland Heights
listening to *A Love Supreme*
unloading bricks of marijuana
far from jungle thorns and the rice filled Mekong—
I suppose his eyesight is fantastic

It is a warm December
and I can see
bare tree branches penciled into the sky
after the snow melts—
when the wind blows off Lake Erie
they rub together with the sound of men
stropping razors

Already the marine and his friends
have acquired a stolen gun collection
spread out on our kitchen table
next to a table hockey game—
a Remington 700 an M40A1 bolt-action rifle
a Mauser C96 semi-automatic and some others—
I worry that after heavy drinking
the table hockey will become violent
because we are drinking a lot now
and smoking a lot
and forgetting a lot

This morning he said to me

there was a section of Vietnam countryside
with cold bubbling water in high lakes
near a Buddhist monastery
where his company patrolled
a rubber plantation
the smell of sawmill smoke
was in the air and candles
he lay down for a minute and slept
in the shade with his gun his helmet his equipment
on a bed of fern shoots
and dreamed of returning home and stealing
and selling drugs because he said—
some men have to pay for high lakes
and deep water the color of tar
and be judged
in the sky's gun sight
or move many miles beyond—
like the smoothest bullet
cutting the greenest grass
like the smoothest skin of a whore
he said—
and that's how Tuesday began
Christmas day
1973

Springtime

My father
pulled our car over
on the Detroit-Superior Bridge
tow boats were pushing barges
in the squat mist of the Cuyahoga
carrying coal to Republic Steel and J & L
on the twisting river
it was another crapped out spring
with snow falling from the eye socket of the sky

Blast furnaces bloomed
like a row of flowers
along Jennings Road
the dust and ash mingling in the air
like birds
hovering behind a farm tractor
in Minnesota
their wings turning over slag piles
waiting for the sun's fire
glistening in the cut hay

Poem Beginning with a Line by d. a. levy

Cleveland
I gave you
poems no one else had time
to write
and you arrested me—
I gave you love
no one else had time
to give
and you
kicked me down a beach
like a piece of driftwood
rising and falling
in the baptismal swells
of your prison hallways—
Cleveland
you beat me
like a poor marksman
tied me to a cannon before the fleet—
but the wind held steady
and my sails were full—
Cleveland
look at me
poetry is a personal matter—
I am not a bloody fist
I am not an animal
I am not a hanged man
I am not a 22 shooter—
I am not the reason scorpions
fight over a kill
I am not the reason bees
swarm without warning—
I am the reason
Cleveland
does not exist
for its own sake
which is something
I've always said—

Cleveland exists as a lie
a necessary lie
for the improvement of truth

Cleveland
I gave you
poems no one else had time
to write
and you arrested me—
before you spread my ashes
beside the lake
I gave you poems—
before the scalps of landowners
were peeled open by God
I gave you poems—
before you were dissected by the filthy
scalpel of the poor
I gave you poems—
before clocks
struck a time of death
I was—
folding and unfolding sheets of poetry
like blossoms
under a cloudless sky

Bill Evans at the Smiling Dog Saloon

Sublime
quiet textures
intricate music
that won't see
daylight—
like raindrops
falling on roof beams
before the wind tangled
the sky in a spring storm
on West 25th Street—
while night wheeled
over the strangled city
the broken sidewalks
the clotted river
choking on its trash
the rain the flood
waiting to make it right

Inside—
between sets
he worked a pay phone
at the bar
fingers nonstop
like a safe cracker
dialing for junk before dawn
wings sweaty
like a sparrow at an empty feeder
desperate to leave
morning's flickering
jukebox for good

Hitchhiker

A soldier
traveling east from Chicago to Boston
in the fall of '67
grabbed me off a road side
after school
to drive his 2 seat T-Bird
to Cleveland as fast as I could
we smoked dope and drank along the way
then he slept
what faith
at 100 miles an hour
in the cold dark
a flock of turkeys
sat in the middle of Toledo
but no matter
I closed my eyes
to guts and feathers
the engine a hot chainsaw
chewing air—
basting toms pressed against
our radiator
as the headlights joined a thousand others
blinking through the smoky BBQ
gone in a minute
like the smell of drumsticks
and the juice dripping
from the Ford's grille—
burnt down to the road
like chaw

Lunch Poem for Peter Laughner

He wanted
to bang out lines of poetry
on an old typewriter every day
at lunch time
like Frank
for as long as he could
aiming for 57 days
to beat Joe DiMaggio's hitting streak
we were talking
at the Scene's old offices
I forget now what street
but it started to rain
wind barreled in
there were many waves
as the lake clouded over
signifying something
I never saw him again
but I didn't know it—
on the way back
I passed Municipal Stadium
in the wipers
like an abandoned ship
where Ken Keltner
took hits away from 70,000 fans
July 17, 1941
zero hour
the night deep as a mitt
at the end of Joe's tunnel
the stands
now a decrepit saloon
a lunch poem
with song and dance men—
he would have said
that's Cleveland for you

Dave McKenna at Bradley's

Around
3:00 AM
he played
I've Got the World
On a String
two at the bar
kissed
and grabbed
they were
drunk
away from home
in separate
apartments
no wife
no husband
for them
the moon
was almost gone
the rain outside
the thunder
so noisy
babysitters
couldn't hear anything
still
heads turned
when he started
Scrapple from
the Apple
in his left hand
softly at first
it's not your fault
she was saying

New Rhumba

He said
a sideman looks for love
anywhere he can find it
like
a cottonmouth
looks for turtles and frogs
in a swamp
it seemed
an odd analogy
we were in Ambridge
rehearsing
New Rhumba
the Gil Evans arrangement
from *Miles Ahead*
he played upright bass
and was much older
a big man
he leaned over me
fingers working strings
like a sailor climbing ropes
assured
at ease
like a cottonmouth
his diet included mammals
birds fish turtles
alligators
he grinned
this is nothing
I could be in the woods somewhere
in a pile of leaves
and you wouldn't see me

I Shook Oscar Peterson's Hand in Pittsburgh

Either
he was in
the Top Shelf
drinking
after finishing
at Heinz Hall
March 12, 1979
or—
I was putting on
a first baseman's mitt
his hands were so big
my wife used to say
big hands means
either
a big watchamacallit
or—
girls laughing out loud
their legs twitching like clarinets haha
better a book of poems
under a skirt to say I love you
and
either
we should get married
in this city of bridges
or—
drive away two-handed
like virgins in a green Plymouth
lost in another chorus
of tin cans dragging
our pants down—
Bye Bye Blackbird
that would have been it

Listening to Earl Hines

How quick
can you write a poem
in the office
listening to Earl Hines
spill notes on a page
in Pittsburgh
before you go home
on a bus
with both hands
swimming old rivers
in your sleep
a thousand times
making the sign
of the cross
in the woods
like a bushwacker
without looking
rolling the road up
in a rug
and a coal pick
Nobody knows
the trouble I've seen
he plays—
faster than
a pair of stiletto heels
on Route 65
before the last stop
hardly breathing
like this
I imagine

Relaxing at Camarillo

for JA and TM

In a far recess of summer
monks are playing soccer—
not marbles not tag not keep away
these monks are playing soccer
these monks are not relaxing at Camarillo
they are not watching the moon rise like a blue medal
over the Santa Monica mountains
over sycamores and sage
these monks are not watching plaster walls and dirty sinks
near the broken Pacific
where Bird relaxed
after setting his bed on fire
and running through an LA hotel lobby naked
his drunken cock swinging side to side
like a saxophone without pants
July 29, 1946—
until the police rolled him in a rug
his arms tied off like a bruised seedling
waiting for the rain to fall
and bloom
like a California lily
like a seaside daisy
like honeysuckle
unwritten
unremembered
as the needle drops—
and his solo starts
like a crutch tapping cobbles
in a marketplace
the air warm
and blinking
as the sun comes up
it doesn't matter
he said—
if you see it right

West Village Afternoon January 1974

I was
in and out
of record stores
dodging traffic
delivery trucks
taxicabs
Christmas trees
thrown out
like old girlfriends
light cords
still wrapped
around last year
as if to say
you'll have trouble
getting by
without me
and garbage
piled to remember—
on 7th Avenue
the Vanguard
door was
open in the sun
like a pump handle—
the sound
of Mingus
and his band
rehearsing
Perdido
downstairs
drifted out
the notes
big as a man's arm
like rats
snapping their tails
on the stone walk

At Smalls Jazz Club

Ralph
Lalama
from
Aliquippa
can't see
cats
crawling
on the bar
at Smalls
to whom
everything
has to be
explained
by horns
until
they forget
to sleep
like rubbery
sailors
their eyes
won't close
over
deep water
until
someone
turns the
music off
with a biscuit
at the end

Inbound

But for me
the bus to Pittsburgh
was empty
until
Lance
was his name
a young guy
pop tarts and soda
in a plastic bag
his sister murdered
the guy who did it put away
all behind him now
he hoped for the death penalty
for his mom's sake
then asked
if I could call his boss
because he was late for work
and the earlier bus
hadn't come
don't they know
people are depending on the Port Authority
he said
before getting off—
this all happened Good Friday morning
I was thinking
he may never read this poem
and the part of his life I borrowed
to cross some water alone

Fortune Cookie

A poet
writes only
to please
himself
that truth
is eternal—
I found
these words
on a fortune
cookie
at lunchtime
downtown
I purposely
saved it
to eat
while I walked
around the Point
and in my mind
I saw the West End Bridge
hanging in the blue sky
like an angel
over water barges
and tugboats
on a most
brilliant sun-swept
Renaissance painting of an afternoon
written there to please me
and me alone
and no one else—
I knew that
but I had to go back
to work

If I Could Write

If I could write
like smoke rising from the Shenango
Coke Plant on Neville Island in July—
like burning particles of benzene
and sulfur stinking as the moon comes up—
if I could write the smell to end all smells
then burn my clothes to a nugget
so when the ovens emptied their fiery slag
my words would tumble out in the finished coal
onto barges and towboats—
the Ohio River would therefore be full of my poetry
with the wind blowing you could read me for twenty miles

Snakeskin

I saw
a snakeskin
in a yard
cut in two like a hose
the men mowing and trimming
didn't seem to care
this was a house
where a captain of industry lived
now old and for sale—
there were crayons in the street
it was summer after all
maybe kids killed the snake
skinned it
cooked it over a fire
ate the meat
and ran naked through the trees
the way the master of the house
once skinned cooked and ate
mill workers at J&L
and ran naked into the Ohio River—
anyway
lawn mowers and tractors kept cutting in the dark
there was no blood on the grass for them
and no words
but a snakeskin sliced like confetti
that blew for hours

Genesis

for JC

I love days when the morning sun
hits Pittsburgh like Billy Conn's fist
one hard blow after another and the old neighborhoods
stagger against the ropes and catch a breath
it's beautiful—
between rounds
the trainers
the cut men
I know what they're thinking
be prepared for a right and a left
a jab about trees and flower beds and hills
dancing all summer until the rains come
and then darkness
like scissors—
but not here
because I command this poem
like God
sweating on the first day of creation
a towel around my neck on the canvas
and a whistle
holding rivers apart
at the Point
because I say so

Angels

Angels
are strangers
bumping into you
a poet wrote—
I read it in *Poetry*
so it must be true
if so
the odds are good
as a city commuter
I will encounter
angels
more frequently
than a farmer
in Nebraska
or a cowgirl
in Montana—
so there are
at least as many
wolves
howling
on the 16A
this morning
when the sunrise
crashes through
feet first—
while the Ohio River
is taking off her
nightshirt and panties
and folding them
one by one
then placing them
by the trees to dry

This Morning

On the way to work
a possum crossed
in front of me
he was moving pretty quick
for a possum
I almost didn't see him
I was thinking
the winter before
I took one
across the river
and let him out
in a junkyard
on Neville Island
everything was included
truck cabs
old tires
all the rust
he could eat
and a river view
then snow started falling
white as the cigarette paper
in January's ass—
when I opened
the trap he ran
into a pile of leaves
like it was a wedding gift from a stranger

How They Brought the Good News from Ambridge to Pittsburgh

He said to her
in the words
of a poet
put your tongue in me
and we will sing
together—
so they did
in loud voice
sharing a bottle
of wine
from Ambridge
to Pittsburgh
on the early morning
Port Authority bus
nearly empty
grinding
its gears
in the dark—
oh stop that song
oh stop that song
it seemed to say
the brakes
scouring
every stoplight—
the driver
coming to the end
of her shift
swayed back
and forth
as the two singers
now drunk
entered the city
arm in arm
that was asleep
and dreaming
even now

Buster in the NBA

Buster's butt
is large
for a terrier
he has big junk
in a little dog trunk
in the old days
he would have been
a good small forward in the NBA
posting up like Adrian Dantley
no one could have gotten around
Buster's rear end—
so what if he doesn't remember
the bad years
the road games
the bus stops
shitting beside the road
in every state—
one time
blind tired
he had to flag down a '77 Mercury
to catch up

Buster Observed

A quiet
afternoon—
the subject sleeps
on a couch
paws sideways
Barcelona
is trimming Real Sociedad
on television—
the football
moves in quick strokes
as Iniesta and Messi
patiently prune this year's
Spanish soccer foliage—
but they haven't
met Buster
cocked and ready
like Mel Blount
running the midfield
in his sleep
peeling squirrel fillets
like pine bark
then emptying
the soft insides
faster than a milk truck
filled with booze—
this isn't Spain baby
haha
this is Pittsburgh

Buster Goes All Hollywood on Us

Buster
is a natural actor
the camera
loves him
he is at all times
an exact duplicate
of himself
his virtues:
his bark travels a great distance
he is limber
he can take a fishing line
turn it five times
and make a cinch knot
he has been known
to get into the hooch—
last week
his agent
found him
sleeping
under a bridge
in Beaver County
wet as an otter—
it will be hard
keeping it out of the papers
this time

The Dance at Sunny Jim's

I am
a wild thing
I was born in Pittsburgh
I am
a raccoon
I am
a groundhog
I am
a fox
I am
a sabre tooth
I move
I roar
I have a radio
I come to the junkyard at Crow's Run—
I break hoods
I rip roofs
I pull radiators
I breath rust
I drink soot
I eat dirt
I talk fast
I am
lucky
you wear perfume

The Mind of a Crow

This much is known—
in high trees near dumps and gullies
crows work together on road kills and carcasses
at the last minute they show up snarling like Templars
their beaks sharp as swords—
other things
they undress girls with their eyes
they find loners and possess them
they are always looking for hard cash
or panhandling
each roost has a thousand wings
like it says in the Old Testament
they make good pamphleteers—
it is rumored they have the brain
of Bobby Fischer alive in a nest
and they tend to it—
they were observed flying in a cloud outside
the great speed chess tournament
in Herceg Novi, Yugoslavia in 1970
when Fischer routed the world
after playing chess all night in the governor's palace
and drinking the blood of his Russian enemies—
according to eyewitnesses
such was his passion
when he became a crow
that his wings beat constantly in flight
he did not glide or rest or sleep
he shunned women
and from that day forth
he would live
in the highest tree
on the shores of the Adriatic
as the ruler of the Turks
as the ruler of Dalmatia
as the ruler of Venice
as the greatest mind
of a crow

Frontier Days

In the evening
we congratulate ourselves
there are no concussions
sprains lacerations
or broken bones
and
bronc riding bull riding steer wrestling
goat tying calf roping and wild horse racing
are finished
it's time for us to ride through Cheyenne
lasso pretty girls and hoorah the town
it's our last night here
in the lobby of our hotel
we see old photographs
of cowboys in long sleeves and heavy chaps
shooting up the balcony behind the front desk
and a picture of Earl Shobe
an outlaw wanted for murder and horse theft
in the summer of 1908
he was the bronco busting champion of Cheyenne
after competing in the rodeo under an assumed name—
we are also competing under assumed names
calf roping each other
tying feet together with belts and pajamas
hanging on to broncos and bulls
in our dreams
books will come later
unknown continents
swimming long underwear
campfires and foreign wars
the moon was rising outside
over the sky's tailgate—
R said grandpa would know
the real name of an outlaw
without even trying
no one but him

A Trail in the Rockies

Nothing
bothers
Old Paint
not the sun
stabbed pines
or the snow
spring hasn't reached—
if my daughter sleeps
in the saddle
he will find
his way
balancing
cold air
like a blanket
so nothing needs
to be said—
and if shyness
is a virtue
invented by nature
so what if he is
a little rough
and rocking
over the miles
from where
we come
to where we go—
his breath bent
like a brush fire
like warm coffee
coloring our sky
written
broken
and rode

Wyoming

He told my father—
coal seams are like peat bogs
like walls under the Powder River
that stretch for hundreds of miles
rock ash forests and water
squeezing into the ground's tight stocking
like a Weight Watcher's ad
and this seam is no slim girl
no New York model with her ribs showing
you can draw a line on a map
from Cheyenne to Chugwater to Douglas
to my ranch
and you'll have a girdle the size of Rhode Island
he said—
I don't know
a man can eat half a sandwich
in the time it takes a dragline
to dig enough coal
to heat a sod house for forty years
coyotes and Indians walked this pasture
and buffalo antelope and cattle
when they start connecting hills
dust and clay and the railroad will get me
not poetry
I don't need money
Wyoming is uninhabited
I like it like that—
he went outside to the horses
stooped over
still wearing chaps
it was getting late
the sun was dropping shadows
mountains and high plains beckoned—
my father slowly backed our Ford station wagon
out the dirt driveway
it was twenty miles to the road
the stars were laughing
like they always do

Passing Through Weiser, Idaho

A sunset
in Weiser
is nobody's business
if you can't see it
if you can't see
mountains at dusk
red and orange rocks
spreading like shotgun pellets
if you can't see lights from cars
and flatbed trucks
crossing the Snake River
and it's nobody's business
if a girl you met
takes off your clothes
while you're driving
grinning like a deer coming to a salt lick
and calls you a jack Mormon
and you leave town thirsty for stones
laughing into a hard wind
like a tramp like a thief
clearing frost from a windshield
with a propane torch in your pants
because it's cold in America
the dry air burns like a banjo
burns like stars flying past a high meadow
doing everything wrong—
fuck it she said
throwing a cigarette out
the window
like a sunburned Italian
fishing all day on a pier in New Jersey—
I'll have to piss in a mailbox

The Night Gene Harris Tried to Kill Me

He played *Straight No Chaser*
at a frantic tempo in a different key
until the piano shook—
I had to keep up
my notes illegible
on the head
my solo worse—
he was laughing
as the crowd at Ray's Oasis
clapped and hollered
while his fingers
swarmed over the keyboard like bees—
I might as well have been holding a shovel
for the good it did
he was laughing
on the way home
I was trying to kill you
he said—
at that moment
I was a gull
high up in the stars
over a choppy sea
no land in any direction
worn out from flying
no compass
and not strong enough to find
a channel a creek an inlet
against the wind—
I would have to become
something else
a groundhog or a possum
anything on the earth
I nodded—
he was a strong man
with thick forearms
a piano string-breaker
up ahead the water was slick

on an irrigation canal
we were in my old Buick
guitar in the back seat
windows down in the dark air
passing ranches and farms
on Five Mile Road
toward Meridian—
and I had heard
this song before

October 1977

To play
a music job in Eugene
I had to get there first
guitar and amp
on a bus from Boise
crossing the Snake River
gears grinding through the high desert
and painted hills
Brogan Ironside Prairie City John Day
before a layover and a joint in Bend—
it was fall
ice bits
in the mountains
rehearsing for winter
caught me by surprise
then a bright morning
sitting on someone's couch
near the Willamette River
listening to *Bouncing with Bud*
I wasn't sure about this
but the poem ends
with the windows down
night expanding overhead
the moon in a rear view mirror
lucky to be warm
and the piano player's
girlfriend saying we didn't sound
too bad
for Oregon

Jack McCall on the Anniversary of His Death, March 1, 1877

Take
James Butler Hickok
for example—
hunter
soldier
scout
sheriff
gunfighter
gambler
actor in Bill Cody's Show
a damn fine poem
of a man
before he was written—
his Colt Revolver spit free verse
like a Chicago bluesman
his back story was A-1
aces and eights
you can't make that stuff up
yet some obituary editors
wanted to know more
wanted to parse the man—
but not Jack McCall who killed Wild Bill
Crooked Nose Jack McCall
who said at his trial
he wouldn't have time for card games
in the future
or poetry—
because
as he said
there are more poets than flies on shit
and in this territory shit ain't good—
he was blindfolded
and hanged
for this insult to poetry

OK Corral

When
my father
was a boy
in the 1920's
Wyatt Earp
was still alive
riding back lots
in Hollywood
a stuntman
with a gun
looking for trouble—
when cameras rolled
he was there
in case a fight
broke out
or when kids crowded
Tom Mix—
once a lawman
always a lawman
couldn't help himself—
at the deli
on Fairfax
old timers said
he sat with his back
to the wall
just in case
or made people move—
he didn't want to be caught
like Bill Hickok
holding a dead man's
pastrami

Colorado

Sometimes
it hits me
the last time
I saw my dad
he was in a cardboard box
at a crematorium
in Colorado
cold as porcelain
before the conveyor moved
I was too late
outside the day was sunny
and everywhere
the smell of autumn peppers roasting
with him
in the high country
on the way home
I carried
his ashes
in a sandwich bag
like a dusty stranger
through airport screening
in Denver
past the blinking heart
of a security machine
who dutifully
examined
what was left
and what was left
of me

II

Floating

All morning
I held my reel open
with a cork float
the line unraveling
in oyster beds and sandbars
disappearing in the mud
where herons stood
in their wet trousers
the sun came out later
croakers and spots ran by the jetty
as the ocean was in a hurry
and pushed everything into the marsh—
it was like driving an old car
in the mountains of North Carolina
the curvature of the earth
on the horizon ahead of us and trucks
and big rigs pushing everything from behind
we could never go fast enough
the car all crazy floating on the tide
like a girl in a cotton dress with the windows down

The Sea Comes to Murrells Inlet

The sea comes
to Murrells Inlet
twice a day
with poetry
spreading
in the shallow water
like shrimp
like minnows
over the mud bottom
the creek water blue as heaven
the tide young and beautiful as the moon
not too high yet but drifting with images—
herons and egrets are out early
in the water
putting words
in buckets
not knowing
their lives have changed

Puffer Fish

A puffer fish
landed on the pier
sucking
and blowing
like a mailbox
fins rough as a comb—
my daughter
used pliers
to pull the hook out
before he could
swallow himself
and things
cooled off—
he wanted
to follow us home
on muleback
we don't live
around here
we said
he had shoes
but no shoelaces
and the asphalt
against him

Goat Island

Goats
move to high ground
when the tide
comes in

Fish live in their bellies

Spots and croakers
crabs
and shrimp
with tiny headlamps

At night
the insides
of their stomachs
glow
like lights strung
in a coal mine

On a boat
you can see
things
moving

The whistle
the steam drill
the workers

The Jetty

The Atlantic
covers
a blind man's
cane
twice a day
but it takes time
as the sea
is in no hurry
to squeeze
between rocks
so the moon
and gravity
come closer
to pelicans
resting
like split sticks
on a light buoy
worn out
from climbing
the top mast
and rigging
on a ship
made of
fish

Breakfast

Mackerel
have been
chewing their way
through bait fish
for an hour this morning
their teeth working the water
like buck knives
in a stack of pancakes—
I have my rod ready
I see them on the horizon
but so do gulls circling overhead
one of us
will benefit soon
from the crumbs
of this destruction
one of us
with syrup
and butter
and coffee
churning

Waves Know

Only waves
know if fish
are there
that's half the fun
not knowing
the line
from my
spinning reel
might fall
in an empty
space
underwater
that's been
cleared out
a construction
site demolished
for future
improvement
a bluefish
on an excavator
might be moving
sand around
on the bottom
putting
safety cones
near my hooks
and sinker—
a lantern
for my
own good

After a Hurricane

A black
cloud of wind
sucked waves out
like a leach
it was low tide
all the way
to the horizon
at the end of the pier
lines went plunk in the sand
like screenwire
pilings groaned
you couldn't find water
yet the ocean
was there
sleeping it off
dreaming
beneath the surface
of starfish
schools of menhaden
mackerel
red drum
in all directions—
but not us

No Luck

No luck
with my rod
tonight
the fish fan out
near the pier
like jittery notes
on a clef—
spots
and bluefish
darting
in the waves
like Dizzy
and Bird
on *Salt Peanuts*
surprising me
like an uncle
way back
who said
if I played bass
and sang
I'd never
be out of work
and was right

New Words

The tide
was running
so I was up
early
with a bucket
and cast net
in the salt marsh
looking for poetry
it was still dark
but I wasn't alone
a heron
took up a position
along a tidal creek
next to me
frowning
and swiveling his neck
I cast
as far as I could
for new words
the net spread
itself
like a rope ladder
and snapped shut
on the minnows
and shrimp
and a red drum
reading Wordsworth
fiercely
in his cage

Pawleys Island

for RW

I cast out
and my line
went slack
in the current
a black drum
swam towards me
with a message
that the osprey
in the live oak
was still asleep
as were the sea oats
and crabs
and what
was I doing
interrupting
the morning
before coffee
and shrimp—
I let him go
in the running water
of his estate
we both wept
a cloud took up
half the sky
and it wasn't
a symbol
for anything

After Hugo

We ate
lunch in
a state park
the Spanish moss
was gone
my kids were little
someone
threw potatoes
in the swamp
like grenades
down a chimney
there were no snapping turtles
no copperheads
on the radio
a country singer
said the gators
wouldn't be here
since the storm
drove them away
it was very bluesy
her guitar sounded
like a lawn mower
on the way home
we saw
puffer fish
riding pick-up trucks
on the beach
raising a ruckus
even though it
was closed

Thank God Robert Was With Me

When a
mackerel
hit my line
the drag
sang like a baritone sax
in five minutes
he was halfway
to Portugal
where the big boats come in
but my son
reeled him back
from his long swim
in handcuffs
all the blood
in his body gone
like butter—
someone
tipped off the law
he said
over and over
again
like in a movie
when
a man
nervously
smokes a cigarette
before hanging

This Poem Isn't About Much

October—
small boats
drifting
in Murrells Inlet
anchors
pinned in
the bottom water
marsh grass
and oyster beds
without end
as the tide runs out
white egrets stand
in a mud canyon
climbed
by fish
like trucks parked
on a dirt
road
we went
through

Croaker Story

I saw
a croaker
beside a road
in Garden City
first thing
Saturday morning
I pulled over
his fins smelled
like turpentine
he looked worn out
he said
thanks for picking me up
the sun rose
over the town
like a lit cigarette
we drove for a while
toward the sound of the ocean
he looked at me
I've been on a drinking jag
he said—
I was thinking
I never heard
anyone say that before
I had to put it
in a poem

Tide Pool

A storm
from hell
took souls
and left
a tide pool
in the morning
at the south end
of our island
the mist smoking
like a bomb crater
we stepped
with our rods
around this miniature
prison
from a distance
plovers
and sandpipers
followed us
in a work gang
singing the drowning blues
singing a jukebox song
about a cheap girl
with a blue dress on
figuring we
knew something
but the tide pool
was still there
when we left
and they were wrong

Another Poem About Fishing

My wife
was pulling
spots
into our boat
faster than
I could bait lines
her rod bent
over and over again
in the shallow water
a quick glimmer
in the tide's circle
and these fish
wanted us
to eat them
in pancake batter
per the local custom
not like
some stranger

The Ritual

When I
feel lucky
I throw a cast net
for bait
in the marsh
I can pull up minnows
and menhaden
and sometimes shrimp
but there's a rub
now I have
to catch something
I am no longer
an onlooker
I'm not joyriding now
I have to open
the tackle box
carefully
put together
a rod
and reel
and begin
assembling
lies

Change of Possession

Bette
is cooking
the mackerel
we caught
in olive oil
and lemon
after the sea
fumbled
and we recovered

Not A Very Good Poem

I can
tell this isn't
a very good
poem
no inspiration
no whining
a silent child
on the page
put to sleep
in its soft crib
dreaming
of waves
and birds—
a poem
like this
should quit
before it's too late
before sunrise
finds the sea outside
slapping the jetty
around as usual
poking wet rocks
over and over
until they cry
for their mother
and will not
stop

Sunset

On the water
we saw a couple
fishing for flounder
in the dark
with spotlights
and spears
going back
and forth
gently
stabbing at fish
in the marsh
at low tide
like lovers—
stars were out
a restaurant
on the creek
pumped music
in the air
like a bubble
from an aquarium
digging
through the calm sand
of the sky
alone now
but not
untrustworthy

Spots Are Running

Spots
are running
so in the
morning
trucks
and boat trailers
are backed up
against a sunrise
like the outbound
Holland Tunnel
on a Friday night
waiting
to unload
country music
and coolers
in Murrells Inlet
the water so full
guitars
and heartbreak
are hard
to carry

Crab Grab

Fiddler
crabs
tune up
in the low
tide mud
the wiggly
songs
of a portable
orchestra
drift
across
hot flats
like tiny
hillbillies
on corn
whiskey
and root beer
my daughter
puts them
in a pail
for bait
whole
families
sleepless
and singing
in her
drunk tank

A Fix

Sometimes
the urge to fish
grabs me
and won't let go
I can't help myself
I'll go anywhere
pawn everything
to find the sleepy pocket
just behind a wave break
where seawater drops
like snow melt—
I'm a junkie
I won't be around for long
no matter what
the bluefish
and mackerel say

Salt Life

It's hard
to catch
anything big
off this pier
as the fish
don't care
if they ascend
to heaven
right now
they prefer
the bubbling
surf break
to bait—
back and forth
they swim
in the rip
pretending
we're not here
like girls
shopping
in the sunlight
for a prom dress
with silver dollars

Tide Chart

Even on
a sunny
peaceful day
the ocean
is moving
pushing my
rowboat
into marsh grass
and oyster beds
or out to the jetty
it's unnerving
like the propulsion
of jazz rhythm
the chords
coming fast
on *Confirmation*
or *Donna Lee*
back then
I had trouble
getting myself anchored
and lined up properly on the guitar
I just wanted to throw a line
in the water
behind the rising
and falling horns

Happiness

I use a
7 foot rod
from a garage sale
a small Penn reel
braided line
nothing fancy
a fish
in the ocean
has to be
goddamn unlucky
to have his name
on my hook—
if I keep him
he'll be on
a conveyor belt
of reincarnation
with the others
high fiving
come back higher—
oh yeah
grilled
with salt and pepper
and lemon
and a couple of beers

Fishing

This is
a South Carolina
evening
perfect as usual
but I haven't caught anything
sunset blue sky cool breeze
and there's a lot going on underwater
I'm told—
the sea
is running with fish
from horizon to horizon
when nobody's looking
practicing for
paradise—
all around me
sandpipers
plovers
and red-billed
oystercatchers
are scribbling
good poems
over and over
in the sand—
more than will
ever be written
by me

RSVP

There were
seagulls fishing
at sunset off
Litchfield Beach
working the air
tracking schools
of Spanish mackerel
in the ocean
with their GPS eyes
then diving for scraps
the spray
flickering like strings
of old Christmas lights—
thankfully
we didn't arrive
soon enough
another day
will be the right place
and the right time
as the party on the horizon
continues
between now and then
and we are
on the list

While We Fished

After church
a blue heron
tried to adopt my son
and take him home
he made a
persuasive argument
with the ocean behind
waves sparkling
the marsh in front
ospreys
eagles
circulating
it was a no brainer
we said
yes
it was
ok

Sometimes

Sometimes
I get a headache
if I'm out in the sun
fishing for long
but it goes away
if I pull something in
whiting
spots
croaker
funny how
taking a hook out
reaches that sweet spot
in my blood
like a line
cast
in my brain
the rig
drifting
with the current
in a shallow
place

I Saw a Flounder

I saw
a flounder
in a '39 Ford
on my way home
by the creek
smoking
a cigarette
and listening
to Spade Cooley
his eyes
were like
bullet holes
in an old suit
he saw the cooler
when I pulled up
it was starting to rain
shit you don't want
to mess with me
he said
my brother
killed a man
but I'm ok

Cooler Music

We put
the croakers
and spots
we caught
on ice
shut the lid
and headed in
past sandbars
and marsh grass
other boats
in the inlet followed—
you could hear the sound
of live music
rattling inside coolers
everywhere
like some redneck singing
David Allan Coe
at a karaoke
by himself—
then everybody
joins in

Pawleys Island 2

A black drum
looks up
at his shadow against the sky
like it's a secret
he says
I'm crazy
why am I standing here
with my rod
motionless
in the mud
as the tide pushes out
and the bottom
gets shallower
and shallower
the creek up around my feet
I'm too easy
to catch
like an egret
balancing
on high heels
and water

True Crime

Bluefish
are feeding
close to shore
spitting sand
along the beach
like a tommy gun
like Murder Incorporated
leaving a message
on good stationary
chewing through bait fish
and bootleggers
like a sonnet
in old school
cursive

Fish Noir

A flounder
walks into a bar
and orders a drink
he needs to hide from the cops
the bartender is drying glasses
by the pay phone
it's Christmas Eve
there's a boat leaving in an hour
a bluefish
at the end of the bar
is doing a crossword puzzle
holding a pencil
like a cigarette
what's a four letter word
for the person who wrote
Autumn in New York
he says out loud
to no one
in particular

January

The ocean
stopped
at a bait shop
to get warm
snow was blowing
like sea foam
the guy who worked there
said they were catching
big poems
yesterday
with a lot of depth
he had a handful of rigs
wrapped in a t-shirt
and a fire going—
a red drum
was waiting in a truck
outside
running the engine
until the sun
came up

February

The sea
and sky
are the same
glued together
minus the gulls
the gray horizon
closed like a shower curtain
everything jumbled together
even bluefish aren't sure
if a line from my spinning reel
is dropping up or down
when they tug
I'm like a balloon
on the other end
of a telescope
my face
in the rain
getting bigger
and bigger
until I bust

32 Degrees

Lines
stretch
like tire tracks
tonight
at the end
of a pier
with shrimp
and chum
for bait
it's windy
hands frozen
the sea moves
up and down
on the horizon
like whiskey
in a still
like a moonshiner
chasing
king mackerel
his foot to the floor
on these dirt roads

Not to Worry

In the afternoon
waves quit
and everything
fell silent
you could hear
seagulls singing old
country & western songs
like Koreans
at a karaoke
deep in the swamp
as the creek
emptied its drain
an old timer
said not to worry
you get these
low tides
once and a while
in river country
everyone's had enough
salt water
and needs the change
a stranger brings—
like a girl
on her way home
from work
entering a biker bar

Nobody Expects

Nobody
expects
to find
a poem like this
in the mud
first thing
in the morning
covered with crabs
and croakers
stroking their scales
sunbathing
snorting coke
and fucking
like Hollywood stars—
but that's why
herons
step
carefully
in the marsh
so as not to disturb
the paparazzi
in the oyster beds
and the egrets
in the water
struggling
with their cameras
to keep up

Old Postcard On Ebay

It says
Greetings
from Myrtle Beach,
South Carolina
across a color photograph
of someone surfing
the cold Atlantic
postmarked
May 25, 1968
Our time is delicious
here...
and no ending
the ink splashed
like a bowstring
across the back
the address
somewhere in
West Virginia
soaked in gasoline—
such poetry
months after Tet
changed the vacation plans
of a mad nation
still
the sun is a shining cross
beneath junkyard waves
blind and carefree
made up
like the newlyweds
on this card
and its report
of paradise
taking their clothes off
in a motel
what they drank
what they touched
drawn without lines
like rain

Wanted

for FS

When she
takes your hand
there's nothing to do
but wait for the end
get a line
in the water
a number 3 sinker
a salt water rig
or they'll ask
you to leave
they don't want
that shit out here
they don't want you
living like a sick hubcap
by the side of the road
like a peach
with a fake limp
rotting on the front seat
of a car
pulling up anything
and eating it
pinfish
ribbonfish
people will look at you
and tell you go to hell
it will be all over
by evening
by low tide
in the marsh
cut your initials
in the pier wood
or buy a gun
that works
you're not fooling
anybody
they know why

Drones and Chanters

A piper
walked
Garden City beach
at low tide
playing bagpipes
his belly
expanding
and contracting
plovers and seagulls
keep a respectful
distance as
Flower of Scotland
bloomed
before the rising sun
and skidding waves
then
Jenny's Welcome to Charlie—
there was no fear
of being found
in this tricky
meadow
harnessed
to a plow
he was alone
on the sand
before God
pushed by
a salt breeze
from the pipes
he blew
overturning
so many
fish scales
like chaff
rising
in the highlands

John Stupp is the author of the 2015 full-length collection *Advice from the Bed of a Friend* (by Main Street Rag). John holds academic degrees from Notre Dame University, The University of British Columbia and Case Western Reserve University in Cleveland. He has lived and worked in various states as a jazz musician, university instructor, taxi driver, radio news writer, waiter, and paralegal. He spends all his spare time playing with his dog Buster or fishing in South Carolina.